PIANO CHORDS 365
BY JOSHUA CATANIA

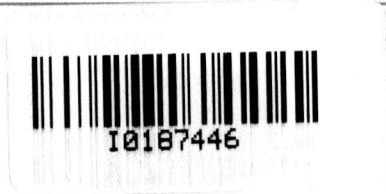

ISBN: 978-1-969094-08-8
COPYRIGHT © 2025 JOSHUA CATANIA & TROY NELSON MUSIC LLC
International Copyright Secured. All Rights Reserved.

No part of this publication may be reproduced without the written consent of the author, Joshua Catania, and the publisher, Troy Nelson Music LLC. Unauthorized copying, arranging, adapting, recording, Internet posting, public performance, or other distribution of the printed or recorded music in this publication is an infringement of copyright. Infringers are liable under the law.

HOW TO GET THE AUDIO

The audio files for this book are available for free as downloads or streaming on *troynelsonmusic.com*.

We are available to help you with your audio downloads and any other questions you may have. Simply email *help@troynelsonmusic.com*.

See below for the recommended ways to listen to the audio:

Download Audio Files	Stream Audio Files

• Download Audio Files (Zipped)

• Recommended for COMPUTERS on WiFi

• A ZIP file will automatically download to the default "downloads" folder on your computer

• Recommended: download to a desktop/laptop computer *first*, then transfer to a tablet or cell phone

• Phones & tablets may need an "unzipping" app such as iZip, Unrar or Winzip

• Download on WiFi for faster download speeds

• Recommended for CELL PHONES & TABLETS

• Bookmark this page

• Simply tap the PLAY button on the track you want to listen to

• Files also available for streaming or download at *soundcloud.com/troynelsonbooks*

To download the companion audio files for this book, visit: troynelsonmusic.com/audio-downloads/

INTRODUCTION

Piano Chords 365 is a daily piano exercise book that provides an in-depth study of chords and their direct application in a dozen different styles of piano playing, from pop and rock to jazz and funk—and everything in between! With an exercise for each day of the year, this book is designed to develop your piano technique while expanding your understanding of chord inversions and voicings, chord progressions, accompaniment styles, and more. *Piano Chords 365* comes complete with practice tips, fingerings, and accompanying audio tracks to guide you through each fun, engaging exercise.

This book is geared towards developing pianists of an intermediate level and beyond to build fundamental skills in harmony while exploring diverse musical styles. The goal of *Piano Chords 365* is to ensure that you're having fun as you practice. If you're having fun, then you're more likely to reap the benefits of completing this immersive piano-chords practice method.

From major and minor to diminished and augmented, each section of this book gradually introduces more advanced harmonic concepts. Below is a road map of the topics embedded in the exercises in each section:

I–IV–V

The exercises in the first section of this book focus on the most common cadence of all time: the I–IV–V progression. You will be introduced to the major triads, major arpeggios, and major triad inversions in all 12 keys. The 12 review exercises are composed in a different style each week using I, IV, and V chords. At the end of this section, there is a bonus week that presents more advanced voicing options for major chords.

i–VI–iv–V

In the second section of this book, the exercises will revolve around the i–VI–iv–V progression. In this section, you will practice minor triads, minor arpeggios, and minor triad inversions. The 12 review exercises are composed in a different style each week using i, VI, iv, and V chords. This section concludes with a bonus week consisting of an exploration of chord suspensions.

I–vi–ii–V7

Harmonic horizons continue to expand in the third section of this book. The exercises in this section center around the ubiquitous I–vi–ii–V7 progression. You will develop an understanding of diatonic major triads and dominant seventh chords. The 12 review exercises are composed in a different style each week using I, vi, ii, and V7 chords. Bonus Week 3 introduces major 6th and minor 7th chords in the context of the I–vi–ii–V7 progression.

i–VI–IV–iv

The final section of this book incorporates chords from both major and minor tonalities, such as in the i–VI–IV–iv progression. Building on the techniques and concepts introduced in prior weeks, the exercises in this section include the diatonic minor triads and more advanced rhythms. Additionally, all 12 review exercises are composed in a different style each week using i, VI, IV, and iv chords. The last bonus week will give you some exposure to diminished and augmented chords.

As you can see, many exciting exercises lie ahead! Whether you decide to practice an exercise each day for a year or turn to a random page as a warmup from time to time, I hope that you get as much joy from playing these exercises as I did from composing them. Before you dive in, take a moment to read over the following section, which contains some general guidance on piano playing and the harmonic concepts in this book.

FINGERING

Fingering is an important aspect of piano technique that deserves special mention here. Effective fingerings ensure that passages can be played comfortably, efficiently, and musically. I have noticed that, when students disregard fingerings, spontaneously changing them or refusing to let go of an awkward fingering pattern, it makes the music trickier to play than if they had taken the time to follow and internalize the fingering suggestions when first learning the passage. It can be tempting to "freestyle it," but I promise you that the effort you put towards following these useful markings will pay off in the end, as you will find yourself performing with more consistency, accuracy, and enjoyment.

The fingerings in this book have been thoughtfully considered and written for you as a guide for positioning your hands and fingers for musical success. However, these fingering suggestions are just that—a *guide*—since fine motor skills, hand stretch, and finger length differ for each player. That said, I recommend following the fingerings as closely as you can for the purposes of this book. The fingerings provided take into account hand positioning, allocation of finger strength, and how to best achieve smooth phrasing. All of this thinking has been done for you! Great, right?

So, when you sit down to learn these exercises, it's important to start playing the correct fingerings from the very beginning so that they can be solidified in muscle memory the more times you play them. That way, you can get right to the good part: the music!

SUSTAIN PEDAL

The *sustain pedal*, or *damper pedal*, is a key component of the piano and its sound. Often, the pedal is lifted and depressed again at each change of chord. Pedal markings have been provided to indicate exactly where the pedal should be used throughout this book. When lifting, make sure that you are fully releasing the pedal to its original position. Pay attention to how this sounds. If the pedal is not fully released, the piano can sound "muddy." With this in mind, you can achieve a smooth, clear quality that can truly elevate the music in this book.

CHORD INVERSIONS

Having a foundation in some basic music theory will go a long way in preparing you for the music in this book. Chord inversions are central to the exercises in this book. A *chord inversion* is a reordering of the notes of a triad so that the root is no longer at the bottom of the chord. A *root-position* triad has the root, the foundational note of the chord, as the lowest note in the triad. The *1st inversion* of a triad is formed when a chord has the 3rd, or middle note of the root-position triad, at the bottom of the chord. A triad in *2nd inversion* has the 5th, or top note of the root-position triad, at the bottom of the chord. Refer to the following diagram to see how inversions are notated. Chord inversions allow for smooth harmonic movement in music, as you will soon hear.

Play the examples below and listen to the difference in sound between the chordal movements.

MAJOR AND MINOR DIATONIC TRIADS

Diatonic triads are the triads that can be formed by using the notes of a major or minor scale. Understanding this concept will give you some awareness of the common chord possibilities in a major or minor key. These chords can be major, minor, or diminished, and they are labeled with Roman numerals to indicate which scale degree the triad is built on. In the music world, chord progressions are named using uppercase and lowercase Roman numerals. Uppercase numerals are used for major chords, and the lowercase indicates a minor chord. As you progress through this book, feel free to refer back to the diagram below at any point.

SWINGING EIGHTH NOTES

Many of the musical styles you will encounter in this book use eighth notes in the swing style, or "swung" eighths. To "swing" eighth notes, the second eighth note comes a bit later than in *straight* eighth notes. Straight eighth notes are played evenly, while the first eighth note in the swing style will be slightly longer than the second eighth note. To keep it simple, the first eighth note takes the place of the first eighth note in an eighth-note triplet, and the second eighth note generally falls on the last eighth note of a triplet. In the example below, the eighth-note rhythm you read in the first two measures will sound as it is notated in the last two measures.

WEEK 1: C MAJOR I–IV–V

MONDAY: ROOT-POSITION ARPEGGIO

1

Our first exercise features the C major triad in root position.

TUESDAY: 1ST-INVERSION ARPEGGIO

2

Today's exercise consists of the C major triad in 1st inversion, with the third scale degree, E, at the bottom of the chord.

WEDNESDAY: 2ND-INVERSION ARPEGGIO

Here, we have the C major triad in 2nd inversion, with the 5th, G, at the bottom of the chord.

THURSDAY: ROOT-POSITION I–IV–V–I

This common chord progression uses a variety of inversions to achieve smooth voice leading. This exercise begins and ends on the root-position C major chord.

FRIDAY: 1ST-INVERSION I–IV–V–I

Starting with a C major chord in 1st inversion, this exercise takes us through the I–IV–V–I chord progression in a slightly different way. Watch out for dynamics and articulations.

SATURDAY: 2ND-INVERSION I–IV–V–I

Here, we have the C major triad in 2nd inversion, with the 5th, G, at the bottom of the chord.

SUNDAY: CLASSICAL REVIEW EXERCISE

For review, here's an exercise featuring the I, IV, and V chords in C major. This exercise is written in the classical style. Be sure to note the dynamics and articulations.

MONDAY: ROOT-POSITION ARPEGGIO

8

Let's begin this week with an F major triad exercise. Pay attention to the fingerings and pedaling markings.

TUESDAY: 1ST-INVERSION ARPEGGIO

9

This exercise gives you practice with the F major triad in 1st inversion.

WEDNESDAY: 2ND-INVERSION ARPEGGIO

Continuing onward, here's the F major triad in 2nd inversion. Focus on keeping your rhythm steady with a metronome.

THURSDAY: ROOT-POSITION I–IV–V–I

This exercise takes you through the chords of the I–IV–V progression, using an arpeggiation technique that is commonly found in pop music.

FRIDAY: 1ST-INVERSION I–IV–V–I

An F major chord in 1st inversion begins this next pop piano exercise.

SATURDAY: 2ND-INVERSION I–IV–V–I

Here's another pop piano variation of this progression, starting on an F major chord in 2nd inversion.

SUNDAY: POP REVIEW EXERCISE

Let's review with a pop piano exercise using the harmony you worked on this week.

WEEK 3: G MAJOR I–IV–V

MONDAY: ROOT-POSITION ARPEGGIO

This week, we focus on the key of G major. Here's the G major arpeggio in root position:

TUESDAY: 1ST-INVERSION ARPEGGIO

Next up is an arpeggio based on the G major triad in 1st inversion.

WEDNESDAY: 2ND-INVERSION ARPEGGIO

This exercise takes you through the G major triad in 2nd inversion. Remember to stick to the fingering markings.

THURSDAY: ROOT-POSITION I–IV–V–I

Articulation is an important element in this next exercise. Once you have the notes and fingerings down, be sure to incorporate the slurs, accents, and sustain pedal.

FRIDAY: 1ST-INVERSION I–IV–V–I

The G major triad in 1st inversion is found at the beginning and ending of this passage.

This exercise features the I–IV–V–I chord progression, starting with a 2nd-inversion G major chord. As always, play with dynamics here.

The *backbeat*, or accentuation of beats 2 and 4, is crucial to the gospel accompaniment style. Also, remember to fully release the sustain pedal when pedaling.

WEEK 4: B♭ MAJOR I–IV–V

MONDAY: ROOT-POSITION ARPEGGIO

Adhere to the fingering suggestions for this first B♭ major arpeggio exercise.

TUESDAY: 1ST-INVERSION ARPEGGIO

Today, we have a 1st-inversion B♭ major arpeggio. Be sure to play a proper staccato chord near the end of the passage.

WEDNESDAY: 2ND-INVERSION ARPEGGIO

This next arpeggio exercise is based on the B♭ major triad in 2nd inversion.

THURSDAY: ROOT-POSITION I–IV–V–I

Here, we have the I–IV–V–I progression in B♭ major, starting on the root-position B♭ major triad.

FRIDAY: 1ST-INVERSION I–IV–V–I

Notice the change in articulation. Connect the first note to the second (staccato) note in this triad pattern.

This exercise begins with the 2nd-inversion B♭ major triad. Focus on your articulation skills here.

This week's review exercise gives you some practice in the country genre. Pay attention to the staccato and legato markings. Also, the chord-roll marking indicates to the player that the chord should be arpeggiated from the bottom to the top.

WEEK 5: D MAJOR I–IV–V

MONDAY: ROOT-POSITION ARPEGGIO 29

Let's begin this next set of exercises with a root-position D major arpeggio.

TUESDAY: 1ST-INVERSION ARPEGGIO 30

Here's a 1st-inversion variation of the D major arpeggio:

WEDNESDAY: 2ND-INVERSION ARPEGGIO

This arpeggio exercise uses the D major triad in 2nd inversion.

THURSDAY: ROOT-POSITION I–IV–V–I

Notice which notes are to be played staccato in this chord progression exercise.

FRIDAY: 1ST-INVERSION I–IV–V–I

Make the accented notes stand out in this next D major exercise.

SATURDAY: 2ND-INVERSION I–IV–V–I

This exercise makes use of the 2nd-inversion D major triad. Note the variety of articulation in this passage.

SUNDAY: ROCK REVIEW EXERCISE

Here's a classic accompaniment style used in rock music. This exercise draws upon the I, IV, and V chord voicings and articulation techniques you've practiced throughout the week.

WEEK 6: E♭ MAJOR I–IV–V

MONDAY: ROOT-POSITION ARPEGGIO

Let's begin the week with a syncopated E♭ major arpeggio exercise. Practice along with a metronome to keep steady time.

TUESDAY: 1ST-INVERSION ARPEGGIO

This exercise features the 1st-inversion E♭ major arpeggio.

WEDNESDAY: 2ND-INVERSION ARPEGGIO

Here, we have the E♭ major triad in 2nd inversion.

THURSDAY: ROOT-POSITION I–IV–V–I

This chord progression includes an embellishment. Play the chord as E♭, G♭, and B♭ before rapidly switching the middle note from G♭ (F♯) to G natural. This can be done either by sliding one finger or a separate finger for the grace note.

FRIDAY: 1ST-INVERSION I–IV–V–I

The marcato markings in this exercise require you to articulate with force. Allow these notes to be shorter than notes with an accent marking.

SATURDAY: 2ND-INVERSION I–IV–V–I

Try to express the difference between marcato and accent articulations while playing this passage.

SUNDAY: FUNK REVIEW EXERCISE

This week's review exercise is written in the funk style. Follow the fingerings closely to most comfortably play the chromatic bassline.

WEEK 7: A MAJOR I–IV–V

MONDAY: ROOT-POSITION ARPEGGIO

This week, we begin with an A major arpeggio. Make note of the staccato markings.

TUESDAY: 1ST-INVERSION ARPEGGIO

Here is the 1st-inversion A major triad as an arpeggio:

WEDNESDAY: 2ND-INVERSION ARPEGGIO

Next, we have the A major triad in 2nd inversion.

THURSDAY: ROOT-POSITION I–IV–V–I

Try to create a wide dynamic contrast as you practice this chord progression exercise.

FRIDAY: 1ST-INVERSION I–IV–V–I

Master the notes first, then perfect the slur and staccato articulations in this passage.

SATURDAY: 2ND-INVERSION I–IV–V–I

Aim to make the sudden dynamic changes as dramatic as you can here.

SUNDAY: RAGTIME REVIEW EXERCISE

Maintaining a steady rhythm in your left hand is key to executing the ragtime accompaniment style. Have fun with this ragtime excerpt, and remember to practice with a metronome.

WEEK 8: A♭ MAJOR I–IV–V

MONDAY: ROOT-POSITION ARPEGGIO
50

This arpeggio exercise features the notes of the root-position A♭ major triad.

TUESDAY: 1ST-INVERSION ARPEGGIO
51

Next up is the 1st-inversion A♭ major arpeggio. Remember to use the sustain pedal at the end of the exercise.

WEDNESDAY: 2ND-INVERSION ARPEGGIO

Let's take a look at the A♭ major triad in 2nd inversion.

THURSDAY: ROOT-POSITION I–IV–V–I

Here is the A♭ major I–IV–V–I progression beginning on a root-position I chord.

FRIDAY: 1ST-INVERSION I–IV–V–I

Try this chord progression exercise with a new rhythmic pattern.

SATURDAY: 2ND-INVERSION I–IV–V–I

Let's play through the I–IV–V–I progression, starting on the 2nd-inversion I chord.

SUNDAY: BOSSA NOVA REVIEW EXERCISE

This week, we conclude with a bossa nova review exercise. Although there is a syncopated rhythmic pattern played between the hands, the feeling of bossa nova should be relaxed. Start by practicing slowly to get comfortable with the coordination here.

WEEK 9: E MAJOR I–IV–V

MONDAY: ROOT-POSITION ARPEGGIO

57

Now we'll focus on the root-position E major arpeggio. Take note of the marcato.

TUESDAY: 1ST-INVERSION ARPEGGIO

58

Here is the E major triad in 1st inversion.

WEDNESDAY: 2ND-INVERSION ARPEGGIO

This exercise features the 2nd-inversion E major triad played as an arpeggio.

THURSDAY: ROOT-POSITION I–IV–V–I

There are some dynamic surprises in this exercise. Make those marcatos stand out!

FRIDAY: 1ST-INVERSION I–IV–V–I

This I–IV–V–I exercise begins with the 1st-inversion E major triad. Start quietly to make your crescendo most effective.

Here, we have a very staccato chord progression exercise starting with a 2nd-inversion E major chord.

Salsa is full of rhythmic flair and passion! When playing this music, it's important to stay grounded with a solid sense of time. To do so, always practice with a metronome at a slow tempo. Once you can play the passage with ease, begin gradually increasing the tempo.

MONDAY: ROOT-POSITION ARPEGGIO 64

Swing the eighth notes in this D♭ major arpeggio drill, and in all exercises presented this week. Refer to the introduction for detailed guidance on this style of playing.

TUESDAY: 1ST-INVERSION ARPEGGIO 65

This is the D♭ major arpeggio in 1st inversion.

WEDNESDAY: 2ND-INVERSION ARPEGGIO

Now, we move on to the Db major arpeggio in 2nd inversion.

THURSDAY: ROOT-POSITION I–IV–V–I

Here is a chord progression exercise that begins with a root-position Db major triad. Make the accents pop!

FRIDAY: 1ST-INVERSION I–IV–V–I

Place an emphasis on beats 2 and 4, as indicated by the accent marks in this exercise.

SATURDAY: 2ND-INVERSION I–IV–V–I

Play this chord progression exercise with a gradual *diminuendo* to the end.

SUNDAY: REGGAE REVIEW EXERCISE

This reggae review exercise has a relaxed swing feel. The accents on beat 2 of each measure give a "bobble" sound that is characteristic of many reggae grooves. Also, be sure to arpeggiate upwards the chords on beat 4 of measure 6 and in measure 8.

MONDAY: ROOT-POSITION ARPEGGIO   71

Swing the eighth notes in all exercises this week. Let's begin with a root-position B major arpeggio.

TUESDAY: 1ST-INVERSION ARPEGGIO   72

Next, we have a 1st-inversion arpeggio exercise in B major. Remember to play along with a metronome to ensure rhythmic accuracy.

WEDNESDAY: 2ND-INVERSION ARPEGGIO

Here's a 2nd-inversion B major arpeggio exercise:

THURSDAY: ROOT-POSITION I–IV–V–I

Time for a chord progression exercise beginning with a root-position B major chord. Keep swinging the eighths!

FRIDAY: 1ST-INVERSION I–IV–V–I

Now, we introduce some accents and more dynamic contrast.

SATURDAY: 2ND-INVERSION I–IV–V–I

Name the chord inversions used in each measure of this progression.

SUNDAY: BLUES REVIEW EXERCISE

Today, we will tackle a blues review exercise featuring the triads covered this week. This passage is written in the swing style, with tons of syncopated rhythms. Practice with a metronome to stay in time.

MONDAY: ROOT-POSITION ARPEGGIO | 78

This week's exercises will also be in the swing style. Let's start with a root-position arpeggio in F♯ major.

TUESDAY: 1ST-INVERSION ARPEGGIO | 79

Here, we have a 1st-inversion F♯ major arpeggio.

WEDNESDAY: 2ND-INVERSION ARPEGGIO 80

Today, we'll work on a 2nd-inversion arpeggio in the key of F♯ major.

THURSDAY: ROOT-POSITION I–IV–V–I 81

This chord progression begins with a root-position F♯ major triad. Identify the other triad inversions in this exercise.

FRIDAY: 1ST-INVERSION I–IV–V–I 82

In this exercise, your volume should taper off towards the end.

SATURDAY: 2ND-INVERSION I–IV–V–I

Here, we have some accents added into the mix. Make a distinction between the notes by playing the accented notes with a strong volume while keeping non-accented notes more subdued.

SUNDAY: JAZZ REVIEW EXERCISE

Today's review exercise gives you a taste of a New Orleans-style piano groove. Notice that there is a rhythmic ostinato in the left hand as bluesy riffs are played in the right hand. Again, practicing with the metronome develops a strong internal pulse, making music with complex rhythms truly groove!

WEEK 13: BONUS WEEK 1

MONDAY: ROOT POSITION   85

This week, we'll explore some common ways that major triads are voiced by pianists and arrangers. Here is a I–IV–V progression orchestrated for two hands.

TUESDAY: 1ST INVERSION   86

Now, we'll start with a 1st-inversion C major triad.

WEDNESDAY: 2ND INVERSION

Let's try beginning with a 2nd-inversion C major chord.

THURSDAY: ROOT-POSITION LEFT HAND

Now, we'll focus on the left hand. The voicings in this exercise have a rich, full quality to them. If your hands cannot stretch enough for the chords in measures 4–7, arpeggiate quickly upwards as the pedal assists.

FRIDAY: 1ST-INVERSION LEFT HAND

Now, we'll begin with a 1st-inversion C major triad. Stay quiet and controlled throughout.

SATURDAY: 2ND-INVERSION LEFT HAND

Next up is the I–IV–V progression beginning on a 2nd-inversion C major chord.

SUNDAY: ROCK REVIEW EXERCISE

Let's end this week with a passage in the rock style, using the voicings you have learned. Remember to lift the pedal completely to avoid a "muddy" sound.

MONDAY: ROOT-POSITION ARPEGGIO   92

Now, we're moving on to the minor arpeggios. Here is a root-position A minor arpeggio:

TUESDAY: 1ST-INVERSION ARPEGGIO   93

This exercise features the 1st-inversion A minor arpeggio.

WEDNESDAY: 2ND-INVERSION ARPEGGIO

Here, we have an A minor arpeggio in 2nd inversion.

THURSDAY: ROOT-POSITION i–VI–iv–V

This is a common minor chord progression used in many types of music. The exercise below begins with a root-position A minor chord.

FRIDAY: 1ST-INVERSION i–VI–iv–V

Try to bring out the dynamics and articulations in this exercise.

SATURDAY: 2ND-INVERSION i–VI–iv–V

This exercise starts with a 2nd-inversion A minor chord. Aim for accurate articulation here.

SUNDAY: COUNTRY REVIEW EXERCISE

This review exercise is written in the country genre. Pay attention to the articulations throughout the passage and remember to establish a solid time-feel with your metronome.

WEEK 15: D MINOR i–VI–iv–V

MONDAY: ROOT-POSITION ARPEGGIO 99

This exercise features the root-position D minor arpeggio.

TUESDAY: 1ST-INVERSION ARPEGGIO 100

Here is a D minor arpeggio in 1st inversion. Remember, the fingerings are there to help you.

WEDNESDAY: 2ND-INVERSION ARPEGGIO

Here, we have a D minor arpeggio in 2nd inversion.

THURSDAY: ROOT-POSITION i–VI–iv–V

This chord progression exercise uses accents on beat 3.

FRIDAY: 1ST-INVERSION i–VI–iv–V

Beginning with a 1st-inversion D minor chord, this exercise offers a different rhythmic variation.

SATURDAY: 2ND–INVERSION i–VI–iv–V

Gradually slow down while performing a *diminuendo* at the end of this exercise.

SUNDAY: ROCK REVIEW EXERCISE

Let's review with a rock piano exercise. In rock music, the driving groove is incredibly important. However, continue to keep the dynamics in mind here.

WEEK 16: E MINOR i–VI–iv–V

MONDAY: ROOT-POSITION ARPEGGIO

Here's a root-position E minor arpeggio to begin this week.

TUESDAY: 1ST-INVERSION ARPEGGIO

Keep the fingerings in mind as you practice this 1st-inversion arpeggio.

WEDNESDAY: 2ND-INVERSION ARPEGGIO

Here, we have a 2nd-inversion E minor arpeggio. Remember to practice along with a metronome.

THURSDAY: ROOT-POSITION i–VI–iv–V

Try to make the accented notes stand out in this chord progression exercise

FRIDAY: 1ST-INVERSION i–VI–iv–V

Note the different accent pattern here. Also, the *marcato chords* will be played short and accented.

SATURDAY: 2ND-INVERSION i–VI–iv–V

This exercise features a mixture of accents and marcato markings. Try to hit them all!

SUNDAY: FUNK REVIEW EXERCISE

This funk review exercise combines the triads you have covered this week. Remember to make use of your metronome.

WEEK 17: G MINOR i–VI–iv–V

MONDAY: ROOT-POSITION ARPEGGIO

This is a root-position G minor arpeggio exercise. As always, keep the fingerings in mind.

TUESDAY: 1ST-INVERSION ARPEGGIO

Here, we have a 1st-inversion G minor arpeggio exercise.

WEDNESDAY: 2ND-INVERSION ARPEGGIO

Next up is a 2nd-inversion G minor arpeggio.

THURSDAY: ROOT-POSITION i–VI–iv–V

The accents are important in this chord progression exercise. Try to make them stand out from the other notes.

FRIDAY: 1ST-INVERSION i–VI–iv–V

Here, you'll get some practice with staccato playing and a crescendo.

SATURDAY: 2ND-INVERSION i–VI–iv–V

This next exercise begins on a 2nd-inversion G minor triad. Try to create a dynamic contrast throughout.

SUNDAY: RAGTIME REVIEW EXERCISE

This review exercise is written in the ragtime style. Syncopation is a signature aspect of ragtime music. Focus on accuracy in rhythm and articulation throughout.

MONDAY: ROOT-POSITION ARPEGGIO 120

This exercise features the root-position B minor arpeggio.

TUESDAY: 1ST-INVERSION ARPEGGIO 121

Here, we have the 1st-inversion B minor arpeggio.

WEDNESDAY: 2ND-INVERSION ARPEGGIO

Now, we'll focus on the 2nd-inversion B minor arpeggio. Keep the fingerings in mind here.

THURSDAY: ROOT-POSITION i–VI–iv–V

This chord progression exercise starts with a B minor arpeggio. Remember to play the crescendo.

FRIDAY: 1ST-INVERSION i–VI–iv–V

Next, we have a B minor chord progression beginning with a 1st-inversion triad. Use the metronome to perfect the off-beat rhythm at the end.

SATURDAY: 2ND-INVERSION i–VI–iv–V

This one begins with a 2nd-inversion B minor chord. Keep that metronome going!

SUNDAY: BOSSA NOVA REVIEW EXERCISE

To review, here is a bossa nova exercise. Use a metronome to practice the rhythmic coordinating required for this piano style. Maintain a relaxed vibe by controlling your dynamic levels throughout.

WEEK 19: C MINOR i–VI–iv–V

MONDAY: ROOT-POSITION ARPEGGIO

This week begins with a C minor arpeggio exercise in the root position.

TUESDAY: 1ST-INVERSION ARPEGGIO

Keep your metronome going as you tackle this 1st-inversion arpeggio exercise.

WEDNESDAY: 2ND-INVERSION ARPEGGIO

This one gives you some practice with the 2nd-inversion C minor arpeggio.

THURSDAY: ROOT-POSITION i–VI–iv–V

Now, we'll work on a chord progression exercise that starts with a root-position C minor chord.

FRIDAY: 1ST-INVERSION i–VI–iv–V

Focus on the accents and dynamics in this next exercise.

SATURDAY: 2ND-INVERSION i–VI–iv–V

This exercise features dramatic dynamic shifts and marcato markings. Be sure to clearly articulate all of these elements.

SUNDAY: SALSA REVIEW EXERCISE

Next, we have a review exercise in a salsa style known as a *montuno*. Practicing the syncopation between the hands slowly and gradually working your way to a faster tempo is the key here.

MONDAY: ROOT-POSITION ARPEGGIO   134

Swing your eighth notes in all exercises this week. To begin, here is an F♯ minor arpeggio in root position.

TUESDAY: 1ST-INVERSION ARPEGGIO   135

Next, we have an 1st-inversion F♯ minor arpeggio.

WEDNESDAY: 2ND-INVERSION ARPEGGIO

This exercise features the 2nd-inversion F# minor arpeggio.

THURSDAY: ROOT-POSITION I–IV–V–I

The chord progression here starts with a root-position F# minor triad. Can you name the other inversions used?

FRIDAY: 1ST-INVERSION I–IV–V–I

Now, we will begin with a 1st-inversion F# minor triad. Note the dynamics in this exercise.

SATURDAY: 2ND-INVERSION I–IV–V–I

See if you can bring out the accents on beat 2 in the first two measures of this passage.

SUNDAY: JAZZ REVIEW EXERCISE

This week's review exercise features the reggae style. Remember to swing the eighth notes throughout this passage. Also, be sure to play the accents on beat 2.

WEEK 21: F MINOR i–VI–iv–V

MONDAY: ROOT-POSITION ARPEGGIO

The exercise this week use eighth notes in the swing style. Let's get started with an F minor arpeggio in root position.

TUESDAY: 1ST-INVERSION ARPEGGIO

Here, we have the 1st-inversion F minor arpeggio.

WEDNESDAY: 2ND-INVERSION ARPEGGIO

This is a 2nd-inversion F minor arpeggio exercise.

THURSDAY: ROOT-POSITION i–VI–iv–V

Honor the accents in this chord progression exercise. Remember to practice with a metronome.

FRIDAY: 1ST-INVERSION i–VI–iv–V

This exercise begins with a 1st-inversion F minor chord. Notice that the accent pattern has changed slightly here.

SATURDAY: 2ND-INVERSION i–VI–iv–V

Staccato playing is the focus of this exercise. Aim for a crisp sound.

SUNDAY: BLUES REVIEW EXERCISE

It's time to review with a blues exercise in the swing style. Keep the articulations in mind here. Practice along with a metronome to strengthen your rhythmic feel.

WEEK 22: C♯ MINOR i–VI–iv–V

MONDAY: ROOT-POSITION ARPEGGIO

Swing the eighth notes in all exercises this week. We begin with a C♯ minor arpeggio.

TUESDAY: 1ST-INVERSION ARPEGGIO

Next up is a 1st-inversion C♯ minor arpeggio.

WEDNESDAY: 2ND-INVERSION ARPEGGIO

Here's a 2nd-inversion C♯ minor arpeggio exercise.

THURSDAY: ROOT-POSITION i–VI–iv–V

The metronome will be a helpful tool for this one. The 16th-note rhythm is counted "2-&-a".

FRIDAY: 1ST-INVERSION i–VI–iv–V

A 1st-inversion C♯ minor triad starts this exercise. Look out for articulation markings.

This exercise calls for a gradual crescendo. Stay steady in rhythm as you get louder.

The review exercise for this week is written in the jazz stride style. *Stride* evolved from ragtime, and its swing-style eighth notes are a major distinguishing factor. The tremolo at the end of the passage is played by rapidly alternating between the chord tones shown

WEEK 23: B♭ MINOR i–VI–iv–V

MONDAY: ROOT-POSITION ARPEGGIO

Today, we shift gears to the root-position B♭ minor arpeggio. Focus on your pedaling technique.

TUESDAY: 1ST-INVERSION ARPEGGIO

Here, we have the 1st-inversion B♭ minor arpeggio.

WEDNESDAY: 2ND-INVERSION ARPEGGIO

This exercise features the 2nd-inversion B♭ minor arpeggio.

THURSDAY: ROOT-POSITION i–VI–iv–V

Today's chord progression exercise starts with a root-position B♭ minor chord.

FRIDAY: 1ST-INVERSION i–VI–iv–V

This exercise begins with the 1st-inversion B♭ minor chord.

SATURDAY: 2ND-INVERSION i–VI–iv–V

Next, we have an exercise starting on a 2nd -nversion B♭ minor triad.

SUNDAY: CLASSICAL REVIEW EXERCISE

This review exercise is written in the classical style. The left hand uses the "Alberti bass" figure, a common accompaniment pattern in classical music. Pay attention to the dynamics and pedaling in this one.

MONDAY: ROOT-POSITION ARPEGGIO 162

This week we begin with a root-position G♯ minor arpeggio exercise.

TUESDAY: 1ST-INVERSION ARPEGGIO 163

Here is the 1st-inversion G♯ minor arpeggio pattern.

WEDNESDAY: 2ND-INVERSION ARPEGGIO

Next, we have the 2nd-inversion G♯ minor arpeggio. Stay consistent with your fingerings.

THURSDAY: ROOT-POSITION i–VI–iv–V

This chord progression exercise begins with a root-position G♯ minor chord. The symbol used near the end of measure 2 is a double-sharp, meaning the note F is raised two half steps to G.

FRIDAY: 1ST-INVERSION i–VI–iv–V

A 1st-inversion G♯ minor triad starts this exercise. See if you can name the other inversion used.

Now the chord progression begins with a 2nd-inversion G♯ minor chord. Note the pedal markings.

This review exercise features pop-style piano accompaniment used in many recordings you might now. Lifting the pedal completely is the key to achieving a clear sound as the chords change. Stay at a *mezzo piano* dynamic throughout.

WEEK 25: E♭ MINOR i–VI–iv–V

MONDAY: ROOT-POSITION ARPEGGIO

This exercise features the root-position E♭ minor arpeggio. Notice the pedal markings below.

TUESDAY: 1ST-INVERSION ARPEGGIO

Here, we have the 1st-inversion E♭ minor arpeggio.

WEDNESDAY: 2ND-INVERSION ARPEGGIO

Now, we will tackle a 2nd-inversion E♭ minor arpeggio exercise.

THURSDAY: ROOT-POSITION i–VI–iv–V

Keep the articulations in mind as you practice this E♭ minor chord progression drill.

FRIDAY: 1ST-INVERSION i–VI–iv–V

This exercise incorporates some dynamic changes.

SATURDAY: 2ND-INVERSION i–VI–iv–V

A 2nd-inversion E♭ minor chord begins this progression. Can you name the other inversions?

SUNDAY: GOSPEL REVIEW EXERCISE

To review, here is a gospel piano exercise. Lifting the pedal is extremely important in this one, as there are many changing harmonies that could easily become muddied with too much pedal. Focus on the dynamics to bring some passion to this exercise!

WEEK 26: BONUS WEEK 2

MONDAY: SUS4 i–VI–iv–V ROOT POSITION · 176

This week, we'll focus on *suspended* chords. Throughout this exercise, tension is created by replacing the 3rd of each triad with the 4th—a sus4. That tension naturally resolves to the 3rd.

TUESDAY: SUS4 i–VI–iv–V 1ST INVERSION · 177

In this exercise, the Asus4 chord is in 1st inversion.

WEDNESDAY: SUS4 i–VI–iv–V 2ND INVERSION

Now a 2nd-inversion Asus4 chord begins the exercise. Can you name the other inversions?

THURSDAY: SUS2 i–VI–iv–V ROOT POSITION

In this passage, you'll see a different type of inversion: the sus2. Now the 2nd replaces the 3rd.

FRIDAY: SUS2 i–VI–iv–V 1ST INVERSION

This exercise begins with a 1st-inversion Asus2 chord.

A 2nd-inversion Asus2 chord starts this chord progression.

This review piece is written in a pop piano style. Suspensions are used all the time in the pop genre. Sometimes the 2nd or 4th scale degree is left unresolved to express a yearning emotion, such as in the Am(add2) at the end of the passage. Listen for the qualities of tension and/or release throughout this exercise.

84

WEEK 27: C MAJOR I-vi-ii-V7

MONDAY: ROOT-POSITION DIATONIC CHORDS   183

Congratulations on reaching the halfway point of this book! Now it's time to introduce the concept of *diatonic chords*, or chords built on notes of a scale. Here is a C major diatonic chord exercise in root position.

TUESDAY: 1ST-INVERSION DIATONIC CHORDS   184

Here is a 1st-inversion diatonic triad exercise. Remember to play staccato.

WEDNESDAY: 2ND-INVERSION DIATONIC CHORDS 185

Now we have a 2nd-inversion diatonic chord exercise.

THURSDAY: ROOT-POSITION I–vi–ii–V7 186

This is a I–vi–ii–V7 progression exercise beginning on a root-position C major triad.

FRIDAY: 1ST-INVERSION I–vi–ii–V7 187

Focus on playing the slurs and staccato markings throughout this exercise.

SATURDAY: 2ND-INVERSION I–vi–ii–V7

Now let's start with a 2nd-inversion C major triad. Can you identify the other inversions?

SUNDAY: RAGTIME REVIEW EXERCISE

It's time for a review exercise. This ragtime passage contains many slurs and staccato markings to watch out for. Also, the I–vi–ii–V7 progression used here is commonly found across many genres, including ragtime.

MONDAY: ROOT-POSITION DIATONIC CHORDS

Let's begin this week with an F major diatonic chord exercise.

TUESDAY: 1ST-INVERSION DIATONIC CHORDS

Here, we have diatonic 1st-inversion triads in F major.

WEDNESDAY: 2ND-INVERSION DIATONIC CHORDS 192

Now, we'll play through the 2nd-inversion diatonic chords of F major.

THURSDAY: ROOT-POSITION I–vi–ii–V7 193

Practice this exercise with a metronome to ensure rhythmic accuracy.

FRIDAY: 1ST-INVERSION I–vi–ii–V7 194

This exercise begins with a 1st-inversion F major chord.

SATURDAY: 2ND-INVERSION I–vi–ii–V7

For this exercise, keep your dynamic level on the quieter side.

SUNDAY: BOSSA NOVA REVIEW EXERCISE

Let's review with a bossa-nova exercise. Practice slowly with a metronome, focusing on maintaining a soft dynamic. As you work up to the goal tempo, make sure that you're still playing the rhythms accurately and in-time.

WEEK 29: G MAJOR I–vi–ii–V7

MONDAY: ROOT-POSITION DIATONIC CHORDS

These first few exercises present a challenge: offbeats. Use your metronome!

TUESDAY: 1ST-INVERSION DIATONIC CHORDS

This exercise uses 1st-inversion triads through the G major scale.

WEDNESDAY: 2ND-INVERSION DIATONIC CHORDS

Next, we'll cover the 2nd-inversion triads of G major.

THURSDAY: ROOT-POSITION I–vi–ii–V7

This chord progression exercise uses syncopated rhythms. As always, practice with a metronome to keep steady time.

FRIDAY: 1ST-INVERSION I–vi–ii–V7

Here, we begin with a 1st-inversion G major triad. Look out for the marcatos!

SATURDAY: 2ND-INVERSION I–vi–ii–V7

Now, we start with a 2nd-inversion G major triad. Stay with that metronome click!

SUNDAY: SALSA REVIEW EXERCISE

Here, we have a salsa review exercise. This one is packed with syncopated rhythms, so start slowly and practice with a metronome. And remember to stick to the articulations throughout.

WEEK 30: B♭ MAJOR I–vi–ii–V7

MONDAY: ROOT-POSITION DIATONIC CHORDS 204

This exercise takes you through the root-position triads in the key of B♭ major.

TUESDAY: 1ST-INVERSION DIATONIC CHORDS 205

Here, we have the 1st-inversion chords of B♭ major.

WEDNESDAY: 2ND-INVERSION DIATONIC CHORDS

Next up are the 2nd-inversion B♭ major triads.

THURSDAY: ROOT-POSITION I–vi–ii–V7

Remember to crescendo in this chord progression exercise.

FRIDAY: 1ST-INVERSION I–vi–ii–V7

The accents are important in this exercise. Also, don't forget about the dynamics!

SATURDAY: 2ND-INVERSION I–vi–ii–V7

Pay attention to the fingerings here—they are there to help!

SUNDAY: REGGAE REVIEW EXERCISE

Let's finish the week with a reggae review exercise. Some reggae grooves are played straight, or without a swing feel. Coordinating the left hand bass pattern with the right hand chords requires slow practice. Make use of that metronome!

MONDAY: ROOT-POSITION DIATONIC CHORDS   **211**

It's time to swing! Use swing-style eighth notes in all of the exercises this week. Now give this one a try!

TUESDAY: 1ST-INVERSION DIATONIC CHORDS   **212**

Let's tackle the 1st-inversion triads in D major.

WEDNESDAY: 2ND-INVERSION DIATONIC CHORDS

Here are the 2nd-inversion triads in the key of D major.

THURSDAY: ROOT-POSITION I–vi–ii–V7

Next, we have a I–vi–ii–V7 chord progression starting with a root-position D major chord.

FRIDAY: 1ST-INVERSION I–vi–ii–V7

Now, we'll begin with a 1st-inversion D major chord.

SATURDAY: 2ND-INVERSION I–vi–ii–V7

This driving swing rhythm calls for emphasis on beats 2 and 4. Give it a go!

SUNDAY: BLUES REVIEW EXERCISE

Let's review with a blues exercise. This one has an energetic boogie-woogie shuffle. Making the left-hand part groove is of utmost importance in this exercise, so spend some time working with the metronome.

WEEK 32: E♭ MAJOR I–vi–ii–V7

MONDAY: ROOT-POSITION DIATONIC CHORDS

We'll continue to use swing-style eighth notes in this week's exercises. Let's begin with the root-position diatonic chords in E♭ major.

TUESDAY: 1ST-INVERSION DIATONIC CHORDS

Here, we switch to the 1st-inversion diatonic chords in E♭ major.

WEDNESDAY: 2ND-INVERSION DIATONIC CHORDS

Next, we have the 2nd-inversion Eb major diatonic triads.

THURSDAY: ROOT-POSITION I–vi–ii–V7

Now, we'll try a I–vi–ii–V7 chord progression exercise.

FRIDAY: 1ST-INVERSION I–vi–ii–V7

This one begins with a 1st-inversion Eb major triad.

Next, we'll start with a 2nd-inversion triad. Use a metronome to perfect the rhythms at the end.

We'll finish this week off with a jazz review exercise. The I–vi–ii–V progression is found in many jazz compositions, so it's a great one to know! Practice the left-hand bassline until you can play fluidly without mistakes, then add the right-hand part.

MONDAY: ROOT-POSITION DIATONIC CHORDS

This week, we'll work in the key of A major. Here are the A major diatonic chords:

TUESDAY: 1ST-INVERSION DIATONIC CHORDS

Next up, we have the 1st-inversion triads of A major.

WEDNESDAY: 2ND-INVERSION DIATONIC CHORDS

Let's continue on with the A major diatonic chords in 2nd inversion.

THURSDAY: ROOT-POSITION I–vi–ii–V7

Here, we have a I–vi–ii–V7 chord progression exercise beginning with a root-position A major chord.

FRIDAY: 1ST-INVERSION I–vi–ii–V7

Once you feel comfortable with the notes, focus on the pedaling and dynamics here.

SATURDAY: 2ND-INVERSION I–vi–ii–V7

This exercise begins with a 2nd-inversion A major chord. Can you name the other inversions?

SUNDAY: BLUES REVIEW EXERCISE

Now, we'll review with a classical piano exercise. This passage has a waltz feel. Get the notes and rhythms flowing before you add the dynamics and sustain pedal.

WEEK 34: A♭ MAJOR I–vi–ii–V7

MONDAY: ROOT-POSITION DIATONIC CHORDS

Let's begin the week with the diatonic chords in A♭ major.

TUESDAY: 1ST-INVERSION DIATONIC CHORDS

Here are the 1st-inversion triads of the A♭ major scale:

WEDNESDAY: 2ND-INVERSION DIATONIC CHORDS

Now, we'll go through the 2nd-inversion diatonic chords of A♭ major.

THURSDAY: ROOT-POSITION I–vi–ii–V7

This I–vi–ii–V7 chord progression exercise begins with a root-position A♭ major chord.

FRIDAY: 1ST-INVERSION I–vi–ii–V7

Here, we start with the 1st-inversion A♭ major triad. Can you name the other inversions?

Next, we'll be starting with the 2nd-inversion A♭ major triad. Try to create some dynamic contrast here.

This review piece is written in a pop piano style. This is a very common style of pop ballad accompaniment. Also, notice the suspended 2nds towards the end.

WEEK 35: E MAJOR I–vi–ii–V7

MONDAY: ROOT-POSITION DIATONIC CHORDS

Switching to E major, let's go over the root-position diatonic chords in this key.

TUESDAY: 1ST-INVERSION DIATONIC CHORDS

Now let's try the 1st-inversion triads in E major.

WEDNESDAY: 2ND-INVERSION DIATONIC CHORDS

Here, we have the 2nd-inversion diatonic chords in the key of E major.

THURSDAY: ROOT-POSITION I–vi–ii–V7

This chord progression exercise begins with a root-position E major triad.

FRIDAY: 1ST-INVERSION I–vi–ii–V7

As always, the fingerings will guide you efficiently through this exercise.

Now, we'll be adding some interesting rhythms to the chords at the end of this progression.

This gospel review piece incorporates numerous triads and inversions that you've covered this week. After all, diatonic chords are a staple of gospel piano playing; they're a great way to harmonize a melodic line in a way that makes it sound full and rich, imitating the texture of a church choir.

MONDAY: ROOT-POSITION DIATONIC CHORDS

These are the diatonic chords of D♭ major. Make those staccatos short!

TUESDAY: 1ST-INVERSION DIATONIC CHORDS

Here are the 1st-inversion D♭ diatonic chords:

WEDNESDAY: 2ND-INVERSION DIATONIC CHORDS

This next exercise features the 2nd-inversion diatonic chords in the key of Db major.

THURSDAY: ROOT-POSITION I–vi–ii–V7

Use a metronome to help you out with the syncopation in this exercise.

FRIDAY: 1ST-INVERSION I–vi–ii–V7

Let's begin with a 1st-inversion Db major chord.

SATURDAY: 2ND-INVERSION I–vi–ii–V7

Pay attention to the articulation in this chord progression exercise.

SUNDAY: COUNTRY REVIEW EXERCISE

Now, we'll review with a country piano passage. Try to follow the articulations closely. Keep the energy joyful and light in this one!

MONDAY: ROOT-POSITION DIATONIC CHORDS   253

Here, we have the B major diatonic chords. Use a metronome to help you with the rhythms in this exercise.

TUESDAY: 1ST-INVERSION DIATONIC CHORDS   254

Next up are the 1st-inversion B major diatonic chords.

WEDNESDAY: 2ND-INVERSION DIATONIC CHORDS

Now for some 2nd-inversion triads through the key of B major.

THURSDAY: ROOT-POSITION I–vi–ii–V7

This exercise focuses on the I–vi–ii–V7 progression in the key of B major.

FRIDAY: 1ST-INVERSION I–vi–ii–V7

Let's start this one with a 1st-inversion B major chord. What other inversions are used here?

SATURDAY: 2ND-INVERSION I–vi–ii–V7

Lifting the pedal completely is central to getting a nice sound in this exercise.

SUNDAY: ROCK REVIEW EXERCISE

Now let's review with a rock exercise. The left-hand part has a driving groove that needs to be played solidly in time with the metronome before adding the right-hand part. If you lose rhythm, then you lose energy. Think of this exercise as the epic finale to a rock anthem.

MONDAY: ROOT-POSITION DIATONIC CHORDS | 260

The exercise this week will center around the key of F♯ major. To get started, here are the diatonic triads.

TUESDAY: 1ST-INVERSION DIATONIC CHORDS | 261

Let's try out the 1st-inversion diatonic chords of F♯ major. Practice with a metronome.

WEDNESDAY: 2ND-INVERSION DIATONIC CHORDS

Here, we have the 2nd-inversion diatonic triads of F♯ major.

THURSDAY: ROOT-POSITION I–vi–ii–V7

This is the I–vi–ii–V7 progression in the key of F♯ major.

FRIDAY: 1ST-INVERSION I–vi–ii–V7

Now, we'll introduce some accents.

SATURDAY: 2ND-INVERSION I–vi–ii–V7

Next, we'll start with a 2nd-inversion F♯ major triad. Make that marcato at the end pop!

SUNDAY: FUNK REVIEW EXERCISE

It's time to review with a funk exercise. Set your metronome to a slow tempo when practicing the coordination between the hands. When you're comfortable, add the articulation and increase the tempo little by little.

MONDAY: C MAJOR 6TH ARPEGGIO

Let's get into some more chord types, starting with *major 6th* chords. Also, we'll be swinging the eighth notes in all of the exercises this week.

TUESDAY: C MAJOR 7TH ARPEGGIO

Here is another important type of chord: the *major 7th*.

WEDNESDAY: ROOT-POSITION I6–vi–ii–V7

Now, we'll add the major 6th and major 7th chords to the I–vi–ii–V7 progression. Give it a try!

THURSDAY: 1ST-INVERSION I6–vi–ii–V7

Next, we begin on the 1st-inversion C6 chord. Notice the staccato articulation throughout.

FRIDAY: 2ND-INVERSION I6–vi–ii–V7

This exercise features accents. Remember to play along with a metronome for steady time.

SATURDAY: 3RD-INVERSION I6–vi–ii–V7

Chords with four notes have an additional inversion possibility: the *3rd inversion*.

SUNDAY: JAZZ REVIEW EXERCISE

Let's wrap up this week with a jazz review exercise. This one is written in the style of a jazz waltz. Pay close attention to the articulations used here. Also, see if you can identify the chord inversions throughout this passage.

MONDAY: ROOT-POSITION DIATONIC CHORDS

274

We begin this week with the diatonic chords of A minor. All triads are in root position. Also, swing all eighth notes in this week's exercise.

Swing ♩ = 110

Am

TUESDAY: 1ST-INVERSION DIATONIC CHORDS

275

Next, we have the A minor diatonic chords in 1st inversion.

Swing ♩ = 110

Am

WEDNESDAY: 2ND-INVERSION DIATONIC CHORDS

Here are the diatonic chords in 2nd inversion.

THURSDAY: ROOT-POSITION i–VI–IV–iv

Now, we'll play through the i–VI–IV–iv progression in A minor. Identify the diatonic chords in A minor, as well as those from the key of A *major*. Mixing these keys creates interesting moods.

FRIDAY: 1ST-INVERSION i–VI–IV–iv

This chord progression exercise begins with a 1st-inversion A minor chord. As you play the quarter-note triplets, feel the half-note pulse to stay in time.

SATURDAY: 2ND-INVERSION i–VI–IV–iv

Be sure to bring out the accents in this last chord progression exercise.

SUNDAY: REGGAE REVIEW EXERCISE 280

Remember to swing the eighth notes in this reggae exercise. Feeling the half-note pulse can help you achieve the laid-back feel that is characteristic of this genre. This will also help you perfectly execute the quarter-note triplets.

MONDAY: ROOT-POSITION DIATONIC CHORDS 281

This week, we begin with the diatonic chords of D minor. Swing the eighth notes in all of the exercises this week.

TUESDAY: 1ST-INVERSION DIATONIC CHORDS 282

Now, let's tackle the 1st-inversion diatonic chords in D minor.

WEDNESDAY: 2ND-INVERSION DIATONIC CHORDS

Here, we have the 2nd-inversion diatonic triads in the key of D minor.

THURSDAY: ROOT-POSITION i–VI–IV–iv

This exercise features the i–VI–IV–iv chord progression beginning with a root-position triad.

FRIDAY: 1ST-INVERSION i–VI–IV–iv

This exercise incorporates some dynamics. Try to bring them out!

SATURDAY: 2ND-INVERSION i–VI–IV–iv

Notice the dotted-quarter-note rhythm at the end of this exercise. Remember to practice with a metronome!

SUNDAY: BLUES REVIEW EXERCISE

This week's review exercise is written in the blues style. Practice the left-hand bass figure first, remembering to swing the eighth notes. Once you can play this fluently with the metronome, add in the right hand. Then, play with dynamics and expression.

MONDAY: ROOT-POSITION DIATONIC CHORDS

288

Let's begin with the diatonic chords in E minor. Once again, we'll be swinging the eighth notes in this week's exercises.

TUESDAY: 1ST-INVERSION DIATONIC CHORDS

289

Here are the 1st-inversion diatonic chords of E minor.

WEDNESDAY: 2ND-INVERSION DIATONIC CHORDS

Next, we'll practice the 2nd-inversion diatonic chords in the key of E minor.

THURSDAY: ROOT-POSITION i–VI–IV–iv

Here, we have the i–VI–IV–iv progression in E minor. Practice with a metronome for accuracy.

FRIDAY: 1ST-INVERSION i–VI–IV–iv

Play a slight crescendo, peaking in measure 3 before coming back down to *piano*.

Now, we'll add the pedal. Remember to lift fully when re-pedaling.

Let's play a jazz review exercise. This slow, melodic piece is written in the style of a jazz ballad. Even at slow tempos, rhythmic precision is important. Practice with a metronome to ensure that you're staying on-beat.

WEEK 43: G MINOR i–VI–IV–iv

MONDAY: ROOT-POSITION DIATONIC CHORDS

We begin this week with a triplet-based exercise featuring the diatonic chords of G minor.

TUESDAY: 1ST-INVERSION DIATONIC CHORDS

The triads you see in this exercise are in 1st inversion.

WEDNESDAY: 2ND-INVERSION DIATONIC CHORDS

This exercise uses the 2nd-inversion diatonic triads of G minor.

THURSDAY: ROOT-POSITION i–VI–IV–iv

Here, we have the i–VI–IV–iv progression in G minor. Remember to make use of that metronome.

FRIDAY: 1ST-INVERSION i–VI–IV–iv

Next, we'll start with a 1st-inversion G minor chord. Try to bring out the dynamics here.

SATURDAY: 2ND-INVERSION i–VI–IV–iv

Now, shift your focus to the pedal. Always aim to lift fully when re-pedaling.

SUNDAY: CLASSICAL REVIEW EXERCISE

This review exercise is written in the classical style. The tempo of this piece is fairly slow, so play along with a metronome to make sure that you're not rushing or dragging. Once you have the notes and rhythms down, add in the expression and pedal.

WEEK 44: B MINOR i–VI–IV–iv

MONDAY: ROOT-POSITION DIATONIC CHORDS 302

This week, we'll start with the diatonic chords of B minor.

TUESDAY: 1ST-INVERSION DIATONIC CHORDS 303

Here are the 1st-inversion diatonic triads in B minor.

WEDNESDAY: 2ND-INVERSION DIATONIC CHORDS

Next, we have the diatonic chords in 2nd inversion. Remember to stick to the pedal markings.

THURSDAY: ROOT-POSITION i–VI–IV–iv

This is the i–VI–IV–iv progression in B minor. Follow the dynamic markings here.

FRIDAY: 1ST-INVERSION i–VI–IV–iv

In this exercise, we'll begin with a 1st-inversion B minor chord.

SATURDAY: 2ND-INVERSION i–VI–IV–iv

Now, we add the pedal into the mix. This time, we'll start with a 2nd-inversion B minor triad.

SUNDAY: POP REVIEW EXERCISE

Here is a pop review exercise to wrap up this week. In the pop style, you'll encounter *ostinatos*, or repeated rhythmic patterns, over several different chord changes. Once you've got the pattern down, add the left-hand rhythms. Lastly, add the dynamics and pedal.

MONDAY: ROOT-POSITION DIATONIC CHORDS 309

Below are the diatonic triads in the key of C minor.

TUESDAY: 1ST-INVERSION DIATONIC CHORDS 310

Next, we have the 1st-inversion diatonic triads of C minor.

WEDNESDAY: 2ND-INVERSION DIATONIC CHORDS

Here are the C minor diatonic chords in 2nd inversion. Remember to practice with a metronome!

THURSDAY: ROOT-POSITION i–VI–IV–iv

This i–VI–IV–iv exercise uses triplets. Keep a steady pulse by playing with a metronome.

FRIDAY: 1ST-INVERSION i–VI–IV–iv

In this exercise, we begin on a 1st-inversion C minor chord.

Once you have the notes down, add in the dynamics and some pedal.

This week's review exercise is written in the gospel style. Triplet rhythms are everywhere in this piece, so remember to use the metronome to anchor yourself in time. When you're comfortable with the notes and rhythms, begin to add in the expression.

WEEK 46: F♯ MINOR i–VI–IV–iv

MONDAY: ROOT-POSITION DIATONIC CHORDS

Play this F♯ minor diatonic triads exercise with staccato articulation.

TUESDAY: 1ST-INVERSION DIATONIC CHORDS

This exercise begins with a first-inversion F♯ minor triad.

WEDNESDAY: 2ND-INVERSION DIATONIC CHORDS

Here, we have the F♯ minor diatonic chords in 2nd inversion.

THURSDAY: ROOT-POSITION i–VI–IV–iv

Now, we have a i–VI–IV–iv exercise that uses triplet rhythms. Arpeggiate the final chord upwards.

FRIDAY: 1ST-INVERSION i–VI–IV–iv

Let's try this next exercise, which changes the rhythm slightly.

SATURDAY: 2ND-INVERSION i–VI–IV–iv

Next, we'll begin with a 2nd-inversion F♯ minor chord.

SUNDAY: GOSPEL REVIEW EXERCISE

Let's wrap up this week with a review exercise in the country style. Play with a light, steady beat. Also, pay attention to the staccato and legato articulations throughout.

WEEK 47: F MINOR i–VI–IV–iv

MONDAY: ROOT-POSITION DIATONIC CHORDS 323

This F minor diatonic triads exercise emphasizes off-beats.

TUESDAY: 1ST-INVERSION DIATONIC CHORDS 324

This time, we'll start with a 1st-inversion F minor triad.

WEDNESDAY: 2ND-INVERSION DIATONIC CHORDS

Here, we have the F minor diatonic triads in 2nd inversion.

THURSDAY: ROOT-POSITION i–VI–IV–iv

Play this i–VI–IV–iv exercise with a metronome to strengthen your sense of time.

FRIDAY: 1ST-INVERSION i–VI–IV–iv

This next exercise requires you to play quietly while using the pedal.

Now, challenge yourself to explore the extremes of your dynamic range in this exercise.

Let's finish this week with a rock review exercise. This pattern emulates the sound of guitar strumming. Play along with a metronome to ensure that you're staying with the beat. Then, try playing with dynamics.

WEEK 48: C♯ MINOR i–VI–IV–iv

MONDAY: ROOT-POSITION DIATONIC CHORDS

This exercise takes you through the diatonic triads in the key of C♯ minor.

TUESDAY: 1ST-INVERSION DIATONIC CHORDS

Now, let's try the 1st-inversion triads of C♯ minor.

WEDNESDAY: 2ND-INVERSION DIATONIC CHORDS

Here are the C♯ minor diatonic triads in 2nd inversion:

THURSDAY: ROOT-POSITION i–VI–IV–iv

This chord progression exercise begins on a root-position C♯ minor chord. Name the other inversions you see here.

FRIDAY: 1ST-INVERSION i–VI–IV–iv

Try to make the marcato articulations pop in this exercise.

Here is the i–VI–IV–iv progression beginning with a 2nd-inversion C# minor chord.

This review exercise is written in the funk style. Learn the bassline first, as it holds the groove together. Emphasize the chords marked with accents, and be sure to make the marcatos pop! Also, practicing with your metronome will help you stay on beat.

WEEK 49: B♭ MINOR i–VI–IV–iv

MONDAY: ROOT-POSITION DIATONIC CHORDS

This diatonic triad exercise uses a syncopated rhythm. As always, practice along with a metronome.

TUESDAY: 1ST-INVERSION DIATONIC CHORDS

Now, we'll play through the 1st-inversion diatonic chords.

Here are the 2nd-inversion diatonic triads in the key of B♭ minor:

Let's try this i–VI–IV–iv exercise beginning on a root-position B♭ minor chord.

Play this chord progression exercise at a *piano* dynamic level.

SATURDAY: 2ND-INVERSION i–VI–IV–iv

In this exercise, we'll crescendo from *piano* to *forte*. Try to keep your rhythm steady all the while.

SUNDAY: RAGTIME REVIEW EXERCISE

Here is a ragtime review exercise to wrap it all up. Start softly to give yourself room to crescendo dramatically in the first few measures. Also, remember to play slowly with a metronome before gradually increasing speed to reach the goal tempo (130 BPM).

WEEK 50: G♯ MINOR i–VI–IV–iv

MONDAY: ROOT-POSITION DIATONIC CHORDS

Let's begin this week with a root-position diatonic chord exercise in G♯ minor.

TUESDAY: 1ST-INVERSION DIATONIC CHORDS

Here are the 1st-inversion diatonic chords of G♯ minor:

WEDNESDAY: 2ND-INVERSION DIATONIC CHORDS

This exercise takes you through the 2nd-inversion G# minor diatonic triads.

THURSDAY: ROOT-POSITION i–VI–IV–iv

Arpeggiate upwards quickly whenever you see arpeggiation markings in this exercise.

FRIDAY: 1ST-INVERSION i–VI–IV–iv

Let's add the pedal to this chord progression drill.

SATURDAY: 2ND-INVERSION i–VI–IV–iv

Here, we begin on a 2nd-inversion G# minor triad. Can you name the other inversions used?

SUNDAY: BOSSA NOVA REVIEW EXERCISE

Let's review with a bossa-nova exercise. To practice the coordination between the hands, first try patting on your lap the rhythm in each hand. Once you have this down, try it at the piano. Remember to keep a relatively quiet dynamic level throughout.

WEEK 51: E♭ MINOR i–VI–IV–iv

MONDAY: ROOT-POSITION DIATONIC CHORDS

To start off the week, here is an E♭ minor diatonic chord exercise:

TUESDAY: 1ST-INVERSION DIATONIC CHORDS

Now, try the E♭ minor diatonic triads in 1st inversion.

WEDNESDAY: 2ND-INVERSION DIATONIC CHORDS

This exercise features the 2nd-inversion diatonic chords of E♭ minor.

THURSDAY: ROOT-POSITION i–VI–IV–iv

Next, let's work on a chord progression exercise. Here is the i–VI–IV–iv progression in E♭ minor:

FRIDAY: 1ST-INVERSION i–VI–IV–iv

The rhythm becomes more syncopated in this exercise, so be sure to play along with a metronome. Also, writing the counting below each measure can help tremendously.

SATURDAY: 2ND-INVERSION i–VI–IV–iv

This time, we start with a 2nd-inversion E♭ minor triad. Can you name the other inversions used here?

SUNDAY: SALSA REVIEW EXERCISE

Let's review the skills you've developed this week with a salsa exercise. Below, you'll see a classic montuno pattern with a tumbao bassline. The coordination between these two parts may not come instantly, so practicing slowly with a metronome will be important at first. Be looking ahead in the music so you're ready to nail the unison line at the end!

MONDAY: E AUGMENTED ARPEGGIO — 358

Let's begin this bonus week with an E augmented arpeggio. You can think of this chord type as a major triad with a raised 5th.

TUESDAY: G♯ AUGMENTED ARGPEGGIO — 359

When an augmented triad is inverted, it becomes a new augmented chord built on the 3rd of the original one.

WEDNESDAY: C AUGMENTED ARPEGGIO

Here is another inversion of the same set of three notes we've been working with so far:

THURSDAY: ROOT-POSITION F DIMINISHED ARPEGGIO

Next, let's take a look at an F diminished arpeggio. Diminished chords are like minor triads with a lowered 5th. As you'll see at the end of this exercise, they often resolve to a major chord.

FRIDAY: 1ST-INVERSION F DIMINISHED ARPEGGIO

Here, we'll play the F diminished arpeggio in 1st inversion. Be sure to include the articulations.

SATURDAY: 2ND-INVERSION F DIMINISHED ARPEGGIO

Now, let's practice the F diminished arpeggio in 2nd inversion.

SUNDAY: CLASSICAL REVIEW EXERCISE

Let's review with a classical exercise featuring augmented and diminished harmony in A minor. In this piece, the dynamics are to be played dramatically to give shape to the music. Start by learning the notes and rhythms without the pedal, then add it in once you feel comfortable.

POP PIANO EXERCISE 365

Congratulations on making it to the final exercise in this book! Today, you'll get the chance to apply much of the knowledge you've gained throughout this book in one piece. This pop piano exercise is arranged in a lead-sheet format. A *lead sheet* condenses music into very basic elements: chord symbols, melody lines, and form. Your challenge is to find chords and inversions in your left hand by referring to the chord symbols above the melody line. Once you have a left-hand part that flows smoothly with good voice leading, begin experimenting with different arpeggios and accompaniment patterns that were presented to you earlier in this book. Then, put the right-hand and left-hand parts together and add the dynamics. Also, feel free to add the pedal if you feel that a section calls for it. Have fun!

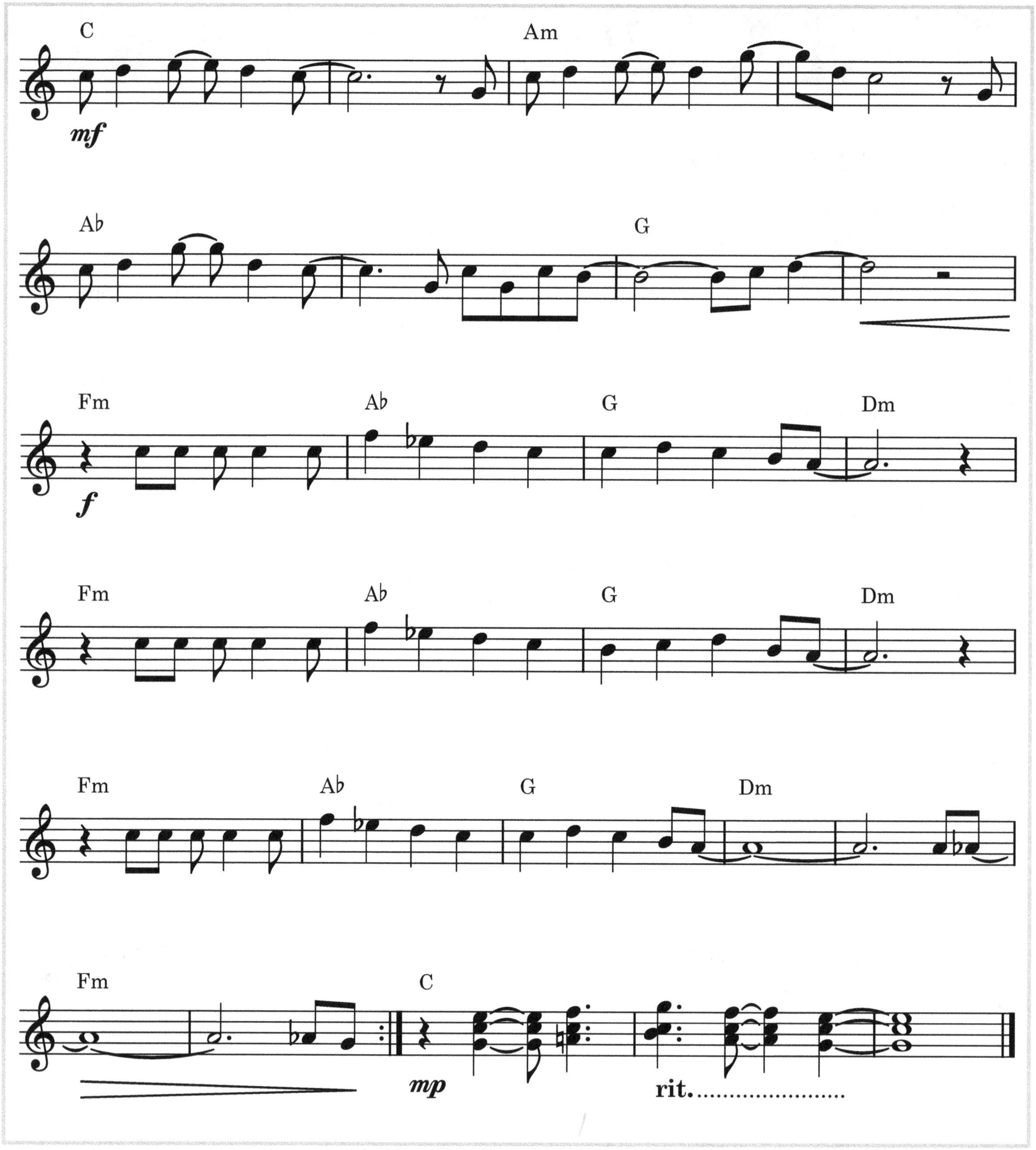
C
Am
mf
Ab
G
Fm
Ab
G
Dm
f
Fm
Ab
G
Dm
Fm
Ab
G
Dm
Fm
C
mp
rit.

ABOUT THE AUTHOR

Joshua Catania is the author of *16 Easy Classical Pieces for Solo Piano, 16 Easy Hymns for Solo Piano: Volume 3, Jazz Piano 365,* and *How to Play Jazz Piano in 14 Days*. Joshua started playing the piano at age 5, and began writing his own music soon after. Influenced by his father, Joshua grew interested in jazz music and began improvising at an early age. Through his teenage years, Joshua kept busy by performing at musical theater stages, churches, jazz clubs, and orchestral halls around his home state of Wisconsin. While in high school, he released his debut album, *Open to Now*, to critical acclaim from *USA Today, Something Else!, Midwest Record,* and more.

Joshua decided to further his education at the University of Michigan, where he studied jazz piano with Juno Award-winning pianist Andy Milne. Alongside his studies, Joshua performed actively in the Detroit area jazz scene. While in college, Joshua also became interested in piano tuning and repair, studying independently with Robert Grijalva, professor of Piano Technology. Joshua continues to perform, compose, and teach in Connecticut. For the last decade, Joshua has taught beginner, intermediate, and jazz piano students. In addition to his creative work, Joshua is a piano technician at a local piano tuning and restoration company.

www.ingramcontent.com/pod-product-compliance
Lightning Source LLC
Chambersburg PA
CBHW081329090426
42737CB00017B/3067